THE · CROWN · JEWELS

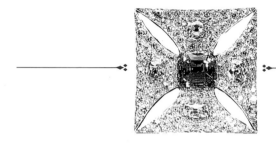

TOWER · OF · LONDON

Text by
BRIGADIER KENNETH MEARS CBE
Deputy Governor, H.M. Tower of London

Paintings in the Royal Collection and the Royal
Library are reproduced by gracious permission of
Her Majesty the Queen.

Unless otherwise credited all illustrations are
Crown Copyright.

Designed by 3D Communication.

Colour origination by Gilchrist Brothers Ltd.
Printed in England by Balding & Mansell Ltd.
(C 500 4/87)

© Crown copyright 1986.
This edition first published by
Department of the Environment 1986.
Reprinted 1987.

THE CROWN JEWELS OF ENGLAND

re the Crown Jewels real and how much are they worth? These are the two most common questions which visitors from all over the world ask the Jewel House Wardens at the Tower of London. The first question is easy to answer as the Keeper of the Jewel House would have been prosecuted for misrepresentation if what he had been showing to some two million visitors a year were replicas! As for their worth, they could be valued purely as precious stones, plate and gold but this would give no true picture. A valuation as museum pieces might give a better answer but it is doubtful whether the best experts could reasonably assess such rare pieces at auction. Then, there is their traditional value – beyond price – and this is the answer that must be given.

The Coronation of Her Majesty Queen Elizabeth II, 2 June 1953

Fox/Keystone

THE
CORONATION
REGALIA

The English Regalia, as displayed in the Jewel House today, are associated with the Coronation of the Sovereign and date mostly from the restoration of the monarchy in 1660, when King Charles II came to the throne. The old Regalia, used up to King Charles I's Coronation in 1625, had been either destroyed or disposed of by Cromwell's Parliamentary Commissioners after King Charles I's execution. However, quite detailed records were kept and a few items came back into the new Regalia. Amongst them were the Anointing Spoon, possibly the head of the Ampulla (Golden Eagle) and the bulk of St Edward's Crown. Various monarchs have added to the Regalia from time to time, in particular, King William and Queen Mary, King George IV, Queen Victoria and King George V. In 1967, the move of the Crown Jewels from the Wakefield Tower to the present Jewel House in the Waterloo Block enabled much more of the banqueting plate to be shown so that the overall collection on display is now larger than ever before.

The significance and function of the Regalia may be understood better by reference to their part in a Coronation. The

Daniel Mytens' portrait (1631) of Charles I. The old Regalia was used for the last time at his Coronation in 1625

National Portrait Gallery

4

first form of Coronation Ceremony in England was probably written in the eighth century and is believed to have been for the Saxon King Egbert (802 – 839). The essentials of the modern ceremony are generally accepted to date from the time of King Edward the Confessor (1042 – 1066) and have remained unchanged to the present day. First comes the Proclamation of the Sovereign to the country as a whole, then, after a variable interval, the Coronation Ceremony itself. At this ceremony the Sovereign is presented to the people who acclaim him or her – the Acclamation. Then follow the Taking of the Oath, the Anointing, the Delivery of the Ornaments, the Enthronement and the Holy Communion.

The Sovereign first goes in procession to Westminster Abbey. On arrival he or she is joined by those carrying the processional objects.

Portrait, artist and date unknown, of Richard II (1377- 99) with Coronation Regalia

The essentials of the modern Coronation ceremony are generally accepted to date from the time of Edward the Confessor. He is shown here in a detail from the Bayeux Tapestry

Musée de la Tapisserie, Bayeux

THE
PROCESSIONAL
OBJECTS

Royal Maces began as close protection weapons carried by the King's personal escort – the Sergeants - at - Arms. They developed into ceremonial staffs carried by a King's Officer and now can represent the Sovereign (for example, the House of Commons can do its full business only when the Mace is present).

In the reign of King Charles II there were sixteen Sergeants-at-Arms each of whom required a Mace. Nowadays, there are far fewer. One Mace is kept permanently at the House of Commons, a second at the House of Lords and a third in the Lord Chancellor's Office. The remaining ten are on display at the Jewel House but on State occasions such as the State Opening of Parliament, or a Coronation, two more Maces go out and are carried by the Sergeants-at-Arms. As Maces were passed from one Sergeant-at-Arms to another they tended to be cannibalised for repairs. All the Maces on display are therefore of mixed origin.

THE SWORDS

At a Coronation the three Swords of Justice are borne before the Sovereign. They are the Sword of Mercy (the Curtana), the Sword of Spiritual Justice and the Sword of Temporal Justice. The Curtana is sometimes known as Courtain,

A Royal Mace

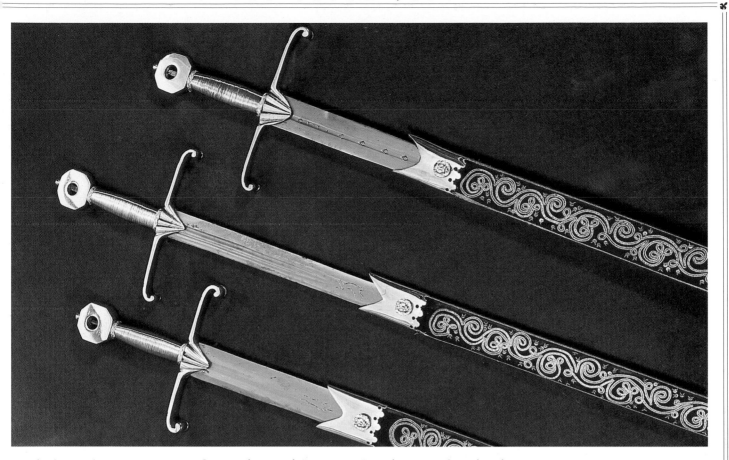

Swords of Spiritual Justice,
Temporal Justice and Mercy

Curtana being a latinisation. It is the senior Sword and is associated with an interesting legend dating from the time of Ogier the Dane, a contemporary of the Emperor Charlemagne (800 – 814). Ogier was supposed to have been about to strike down a son of Charlemagne in revenge for the murder of his own son when the Angel of the Lord appeared and struck his sword aside, breaking the end of it and saying "Mercy is better than revenge". Consequently, the Sword of Mercy always has a broken end.

The three swords were made for the Coronation of King Charles II in 1661. They were given new hilts for the Coronation of King James II in 1685. The blades are older, probably late sixteenth century. On the Sword of Spiritual Justice the 'running wolf' mark used by the German swordsmiths of Passau and Solingen can be clearly seen.

Also carried in procession is the Great Sword of State, symbolising the Sovereign's personal sword. It is a two-handed sword of seventeenth-century design, first used at

The Great Sword of State, 1678

St. Edward's Staff, 1661

the Coronation of King James II. It is also used at the State Opening of Parliament and is normally carried by a senior retired sailor, soldier or airman nominated by the Queen. A second Sword of State, the former Irish Sword of State and no longer used, was probably carried at the Coronation of King Charles II. It left England in 1685 and returned in 1922 on the formation of the Irish Free State.

ST EDWARD'S STAFF

St Edward's Staff is a long, gold sceptre with a Cross on the top and a steel tip. It is carried in procession before the Sovereign and laid on the altar at Westminster Abbey where it remains and takes no further part in the ceremony. Its symbolism is obscure. Perhaps it can best be likened to the pastoral staff of a bishop.

THE TRUMPETS

There are sixteen State Trumpets, of which only ten are on display. Of solid silver they have not been used since the middle of the last century when the Corps of civilian State

Sir Godfrey Kneller's portrait (1684-85) of James II. The Great Sword of State was first used at his Coronation in 1685

A State Trumpet

Trumpeters was disbanded as an economy measure by the Duke of Wellington. The trumpets used today are of silver plate. Those on display date from the period between 1780 and 1848. They cannot be played with their present mouth pieces, which are drilled and not properly fashioned. The original mouth pieces were retained by the trumpeters as their personal property, according to tradition. At a Coronation, the trumpeters come from the Household Cavalry, using their own instruments.

THE
ANOINTING
OBJECTS

After the procession comes the Acclamation, following which the Sovereign takes the oath and sits in the Chair of State. The Archbishop of Canterbury begins the Service of Holy Communion which is interrupted after the Creed for the first Coronation Ceremony of Anointing. The Sovereign is divested of the crimson robes and leaves the Chair of State to sit in King Edward's Chair. The holy oil is poured from the Ampulla into the Anointing Spoon and the Archbishop touches the Sovereign on hands, breast and crown of head. The Ampulla is in the form of an eagle and dates from the Coronation of King Charles II. It is made of gold but the head is not of the same period as it has a fourteenth-century screw-thread.

The old Ampulla was jewelled and probably broken up or stolen at the time of the disposal of the Crown Jewels under Cromwell. It is conjectured that one of the clergy may have unscrewed the old head and retained it until the Restoration when it was given back to be joined with the new body. Known weights and costs of the replacement body and head tend to support this story.

The Spoon is the oldest piece of the Regalia and dates from the twelfth century. The handle is probably some sixty years older than the bowl and it is thought that it was first used at the Coronation of King John in 1199. The bowl of the Spoon has the same pattern as a small chalice found in Canterbury in the tomb of Archbishop Hubert Walter who crowned King John. Apart from four small pearls added at the time of the Coronation of King William and Queen Mary in 1689 and its re-gilding, it is virtually in the original state, although it may have been enamelled in colours in the Middle Ages.

The Ampulla and Spoon

T H E
ORNAMENTS

At this stage in the Ceremony the Sovereign is invested with the Coronation Robes and the Ornaments, preparatory to the Crowning. The Coronation Robes consist of a Supertunica or Dalmatic, a Pallium Regale or Imperial Mantle, a Stole and a Girdle. The Supertunica is a copy of a Roman Consul's dress uniform. Both it and the accompanying Mantle were made of gold thread for the Coronation of King George IV in 1821. Together they weigh some 23 lb (10 kg). King George IV wore the Mantle but not the Supertunica, which he thought too feminine, preferring his uniform boots and breeches. Queen Victoria could not wear the Robes at her Coronation in 1838 because she was much too small for them. However, normally our Sovereigns, including Queen Elizabeth II, have worn the Robes at their Coronation.

The Stole was given to Queen Elizabeth II by Commonwealth nations of which she was then titular head at her Coronation in 1953. The floral emblems on it symbolise Sri Lanka, India, New Zealand, Australia, Canada, Ireland, Wales, Scotland and England. For Wales the leek is used as the daffodil would not show up well on gold thread. Also shown on the Stole are St Edward's Crown, the Imperial Eagle, the Holy Ghost represented by a dove, the flags of St Patrick, St Andrew and St George and the insignia of the saints Matthew, Mark, Luke, John and Peter.

The Stole, 1953

⤙ SPURS AND SWORD ⤚

The Golden Spurs, signifying knighthood, are brought from the altar and are applied for a moment to the Sovereign's heels before being replaced upon the altar. Although the

Spurs were made for the Coronation of King Charles II and are of seventeenth-century style, they are of the old pre-thirteenth-century design with a single point at the heel.

The Sovereign's personal Sword is then delivered to the accompaniment of an impressive exhortation, after which the Sovereign ungirds the Sword and offers it upon the altar. It is later redeemed in the sum of 100 shillings and carried unsheathed before the Sovereign. The Sword, made in 1820, is magnificently jewelled and has a scabbard of solid gold and a blade of damask steel. It is one of the most expensive swords in the world.

⤙ ARMILLS, ORB AND CORONATION RINGS ⤚

Then follows the investing with the Armills, the bracelets of sincerity and wisdom. On display in the Jewel House are the Armills made for the Coronation of King Charles II, although it is doubtful whether he wore them. They are beautifully enamelled. Queen Elizabeth II was presented by the Commonwealth nations with new Armills of gold made

The Golden Spurs, 1661

The Imperial Mantle, 1821

The Supertunica, 1821

The Jewelled State Sword, 1820

for her by Garrard's, the present Crown Jewellers. They have a Tudor Rose clasp.

The Orb is now placed by the Archbishop into the Sovereign's right hand and is then returned to the altar. It is a hollow gold sphere, 6½ in (165 mm) in diameter, made for the Coronation of King Charles II, and weighs 2 lb 14 oz (1.3 kg). It symbolises the Christian sovereignty over the earth, the Sovereign being the head of the Anglican Church.

A second Orb was made for Queen Mary II. When King William and Queen Mary came to the throne they were each treated as King and Queen in their own right. Consequently, two sets of personal Regalia were made. The second Orb was used at the Coronations of Queen Anne (1702), King George I (1714), King George II (1727) and King George III (1761) but when King George IV came to the throne he decided to revert to the slightly larger King Charles II Orb which has been in use for all subsequent Coronations. Both Orbs

The Armills, 1953

The Sovereign's Orb, 1661 and Queen Mary II's Orb, 1689

Sir William Beechey's portrait (c1831) of Queen Adelaide. The Queen Consort's Ring was made for her for the Coronation in 1831 of her husband, William IV

were placed on the coffin of Queen Victoria at her funeral.

The Sovereign's Ring is then placed on the fourth finger of the Sovereign's right hand. The Ring is that made for King William IV in 1831. Before that time, both the Sovereign's Ring and the Queen Consort's Ring were the personal property of the King and Queen concerned and new ones were made for each Coronation. Nowadays, the Sovereign's Ring and the Queen Consort's Ring, which was made for Queen Adelaide, wife of King William IV, remain part of the Regalia. The Sovereign's Ring is sometimes known as the "Wedding Ring of England".

Also on display is a much smaller Coronation Ring, made for Queen Victoria and given to her by her mother, the Duchess of Kent. The existing Coronation Ring could not be adjusted to fit Queen Victoria's small fingers. Unfortunately, the jeweller made the Ring for the little finger instead of the fourth finger of the right hand. The confusion was caused by the use of the new finger count. On the old count, the position

The Sovereign's Ring, 1831 and the Queen Consort's Ring, 1831

of a ring would be described as the fourth finger of the right hand, on the new as the third finger of the right hand. Although the Archbishop was aware of the problem he insisted on forcing the Ring on to the correct finger at Queen Victoria's Coronation. It is said that it took two hours and much ice to remove it!

John Michael Wright's portrait (c1661) of Charles II. The Sceptre with the Cross was made for his Coronation in 1661

✦ THE SCEPTRES ✦

Following the Ring, the Sovereign is invested with the Sceptre with the Cross and the Sceptre with the Dove. The Sceptre with the Cross symbolises the Sovereign's temporal power as the ruler of his or her people. It was made for the Coronation of King Charles II but partly re-made in 1910 to receive the largest cut diamond in the world, the First Star of Africa, which weighs some 530 carats. This diamond came from the Cullinan Diamond, found in the Premier Mine in South Africa in 1905 by an African mine worker who summoned the Mine Superintendent, Frederick Wells. The Transvaal Government presented it to King Edward VII in 1907 on his sixty-sixth birthday. It weighed 3,106 carats and was cut into nine major and ninety-six minor diamonds. The largest two stones, the First and Second Stars of Africa, form part of the Crown Jewels and are also the two largest cut diamonds in the world. The next seven belong personally to Queen Elizabeth II.

The Sceptre with the Dove, also made for the Coronation of King Charles II, has a rather vague symbolism. The Dove on top represents the Holy Ghost and, overall, the Sceptre represents the Sovereign's regal authority in the sense of equity and mercy.

✦ ST EDWARD'S CROWN ✦

Now comes the climax of the Coronation when the Archbishop places St Edward's Crown on the Sovereign's head and the Sovereign is acclaimed by the congregation. St Edward's Crown is made of gold and is very heavy, weighing an ounce under 5 lb (2.3 kg);. It is set with semi-precious stones which are of no great significance as it was one of the crowns which used to be re-set with stones for each Coronation. The stones were hired from a jeweller and returned afterwards, leaving the crown to be set with crystals for display. The present stones were set in the Crown in 1910 for King George V's Coronation and have remained ever since. The Crown dates from the Coronation of King Charles II but records show that it was an old crown refurbished. It is highly probable that it was one of three old crowns held at

The Sceptre with the Cross

The Sceptre with the Dove – the Rod of Equity, 1661

St. Edward's Crown

Chalices and Patens, c1650

Westminster Abbey before the Cromwellian Commonwealth. From records of the costs and weight it is possible that at least the lower half of the Crown may have been that of King Edward the Confessor, the alterations being centred on the arches.

—•: COMMUNION PLATE AND ALTAR DISH :•—

There are five Communion vessels in gold, comprising two chalices and three patens. They were used first at the Coronation of King Charles II. All are engraved with the Arms of King William and Queen Mary. In addition, there is a very large Altar Dish, some 37 in (940 mm) in diameter which forms the centrepiece of the altar at Westminster Abbey at a Coronation and shows the Last Supper. It was made in 1664 and the maker's initials were HG. His full name is not known as the records were lost in the Great Fire of London in 1666. After the Communion the Sovereign descends from the throne and withdraws to be dressed for departure. St Edward's Crown is then replaced by the Imperial State Crown.

Altar Dish, 1664

Imperial State Crown (front)

Imperial State Crown (back)

◆→ THE IMPERIAL STATE CROWN ◆—

This Crown is the best known of all the State Regalia. It is worn by the Sovereign not only on leaving Westminster Abbey after a Coronation but also on major State occasions, such as the State Opening of Parliament.

The present Crown was designed and made for Queen Victoria in 1837 and re-made by the present Crown Jewellers for King George VI in 1937. For the Coronation of Queen Elizabeth II in 1953 the shape of the arches was altered to reduce the total height. Although more than 2,800 diamonds are mounted in it, it is perhaps most famous for its major precious stones, precious either for their historical interest or their actual value. In the Maltese Cross at the top is a sapphire said to have come from the ring of King Edward the Confessor when he was re-interred in Westminster Abbey by King Henry II in 1163.

Under the monde at the top of the Crown there are four very large, old, drop pearls. They may have come from twin ear-rings of Queen Elizabeth I or, possibly, from those of Elizabeth of Bohemia, the daughter of King James I. When they were transferred from the previous Imperial State

Portrait (c1610) after Nicholas Hilliard of Mary Queen of Scots, who was a former owner of the collection now known as the Hanoverian Pearls

Portrait, artist and date unknown, of Elizabeth I, who bought the Hanoverian Pearls on the death of Mary Queen of Scots

Crown in 1837 there were only three pearls; the fourth was supplied by the Crown Jewellers of the day, Rundell, Bridge & Rundell. At least three of the pearls may have come from the collection now generally known as the Hanoverian Pearls. These pearls have a romantic history. They were given by Pope Clement VII to Catherine de Medici and by her to Mary Queen of Scots in 1559 when she married the Dauphin of France, Catherine de Medici's son. At this time they consisted of six long strings of pearls, twenty-five, described in a letter by the French Ambassador of the day, de la Forêt, as being "as large as nutmegs". In addition, there were seven large separate pearls which may have been used in ear-rings or brooches.

After the execution of Mary Queen of Scots, Queen Elizabeth I bought the pearls on valuation and they passed in succession to King James I who gave them to his daughter, Elizabeth of Bohemia. On her death, they went to her daughter Sophia, the Electress of Hanover, and then in succession from Sophia's son, who became King George I, right through to the present day when both Queen Elizabeth and Queen Elizabeth the Queen Mother have necklaces made from those pearls.

The next stone of note is the Black Prince's Ruby. It is not a true ruby but a balas or spinel, a semi-precious stone.

Her Majesty the Queen wearing the Imperial State Crown and holding the Sceptre with the Cross and the Sovereign's Orb. Photographed by Cecil Beaton, 1953

Royal Collection

Portrait, artist and date unknown, of Henry V, who wore the Black Prince's Ruby, now part of the Imperial State Crown, at the Battle of Agincourt in 1415

It is pierced in the oriental style and is of great historic value. It was always considered lucky to have a red stone in the Crown and this spinel has a long history. It was owned by the Moors before it came into the hands of Pedro the Cruel, King of Castile, who gave it to the Black Prince, son of King Edward III, in gratitude after the Battle of Najera in 1367. King Henry V wore it at the Battle of Agincourt in 1415 but nearly lost it when he was hit on the side of the head in a charge led by the Duc d'Alençon.

Underneath this large spinel is the second largest diamond in the world, the Second Star of Africa, which weighs some 317 carats. This diamond and the First Star of Africa, which is in the head of the Sceptre, can be clipped together to form a brooch. Queen Mary, wife of King George V, occasionally wore them in this manner.

At the back of the Crown is the Stuart Sapphire, a very large sapphire of some 104 carats. Its history before the time of King Charles II is obscure. Probably in the Scottish Crown at the Coronation of King Alexander II in 1214, it may well have come into the hands of King Edward I at the same time as the Stone of Scone. It passed back into Scottish hands as a gift from King Edward III to King David II and thereafter was owned by the Stuart family. It left England with King James II in 1688 and eventually returned to the Regalia after the death of the last of the Stuarts, Henry Cardinal York, in 1807. It used to be set in the front of the Imperial State Crown until the acquisition of the Second Star of Africa.

Top (left to right): First Star of Africa and the Stuart Sapphire. Bottom (left to right): Koh-i-noor and the Second Star of Africa

❖ CONSORT'S REGALIA ❖

When the King's Consort is crowned with him she is given a simpler version of the Sceptre with the Cross, but instead of the Sceptre with the Dove, she carries the Ivory Rod. Both were made for the Coronation of Mary of Modena, wife of King James II, and have been used regularly since then except in 1689 when King William and Queen Mary were each invested with their own Ornaments.

The Queen Consort's Ivory Rod and the Queen Consort's Sceptre

Case 5	Case 6

Case 4

Case 3

Case 2

Case 1

GROUND FLOOR PLAN

Case 1
Wine cooler, 1829, and ladle, 1841
Two dish warmers and covers c1820

Case 2
Thirteen maces (The House of
Commons mace and the two Lord
Chancellor's maces are in use)
The Sword of State, 1678
The Sword of State, 17th century

Case 3
Two flagons, 1664
Two candlesticks, c1662
Two flagons, c1660
Two flagons, 1660
Two altar dishes, c1661

Case 4
Ten State trumpets, 1780-1848
The Victoria Cross, the George Cross
The Orders of Merit (Civil and
Military Divisions)
The Companionate of Honour
The Order of the Garter, KG
The Order of the Thistle, KT
The Order of the Bath
The Order of St Michael and St George
The Royal Victorian Order
The Order of the British Empire
The Order of St Patrick
The Order of the Star of India
The Order of the Crown of India
The Order of the Indian Empire

Case 5
Robes:
The Order of the British Empire
Knight Grand Cross, GBE
The Royal Victorian Order
Knight Grand Cross, GCVO
The Order of St Michael and St George
Knight Grand Cross, GCMG
The Order of the Bath
Knight Grand Cross, GCB
The Order of the Thistle
The Order of the Garter

Case 6
The Sovereign's Coronation robes,
Dalmatic and the Imperial mantle

BASEMENT FLOOR PLAN

1 Lily christening font, 1840
2 Ewer, c1735
3 Basin, c1735
4 Sword of Spiritual Justice
5 The Exeter Salt, c1630
6 Orb of Mary II, 1689
7 Prince of Wales Crown, 1728
8 Monde from the old crown of
  James II, 1685
9 Crown of Mary of Modena, 1685
10 Diadem of Mary of Modena, 1685
11 Sceptre with the Dove, the Rod of
  Equity (Mary II, 1689)
12 Bracelets, Charles II, 1661

13 Queen Consort's Sceptre with the
  Cross, 1685
14 Prince of Wales Crown, 1901
15 Two tankards, c1650
16 Fountain and perfume burner,
  c1650
17 Four standing salts, c1661
18 Crown worn by George V at the
  Delhi Durbar in 1911
19 Crown of Queen Elizabeth the
  Queen Mother, 1937
20 Crown of Queen Mary, Consort of
  George V, 1911
21 Queen Victoria's small crown,
  1870

22 Queen Consort's Ring and Queen
  Victoria's Coronation Ring
23 Gold chalice and paten, c1661
24 Gold paten, c1661
25 The Queen Consort's Ivory Rod
26 Original armlet with model of the
  Koh-i-Noor diamond
27 Standing salt, called after Elizabeth
  I, 1572
28 Seven standing salts, Charles II,
  1661
29 Twelve salt spoons, George IV, 1820
30 Altar dish, 1664
31 Two flagons, c1661
32 Two stand patens, 1714 and 1736

THE
CROWN JEWELS
AND PLATE IN THE JEWEL HOUSE

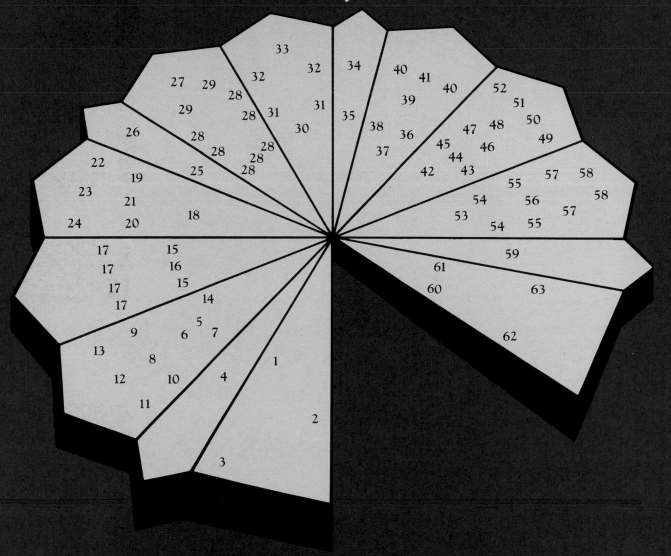

33 Altar dish, 1660
34 Sword of Temporal Justice
35 Model of the uncut Cullinan diamond
36 Altar dish, Charles II, 1660
37 Christening font, Charles II, 1660
38 Alms dish, cypher Queen Anne, 1660
39 St Edward's Staff, Charles II, 1661
40 Two chalices, Charles II, 1660 and 1664
41 Pitcher, William and Mary, 1692
42 St Edward's Crown, the coronation crown, 1661
43 Ampulla and spoon

44 The Imperial State Crown of Elizabeth II, 1953
45 The Sovereign's Orb, 1661
46 The armills of Elizabeth II, 1953
47 St George's Spurs, 1661
48 Sceptre with the Cross, 1661, with the Star of Africa (Cullinan) diamond
49 Sceptre with the Dove, Rod of Equity, 1661
50 Gold chalice and paten, 1661
51 The Coronation Ring, 1831
52 The Jewelled State Sword, 1820
53 The Maundy Dish, 1660
54 Maundy money

55 Two flagons, 1664
56 Flagon, cypher Queen Anne, 1660
57 Two patens, 1698 and 1702
58 Two stand patens, 1664
59 Curtana, or the Sword of Mercy
60 Alms dish, cypher William and Mary, 1691
61 Flagon, cypher William and Mary, 1691
62 Caddinet and vinegar jug, cypher William and Mary, 1683
63 Caddinet and vinegar jug, cypher William and Mary, 1689

THE
OTHER
CROWNS

Constitutional practice forbids the crowns of England to leave the country. The ban was probably to prevent Sovereigns from selling or pawning the Crown Jewels to help pay for overseas campaigns. Consequently, when a crown was required for the Delhi Durbar in 1911, the Maharajahs of India sent some exquisite precious stones to the present Crown Jewellers for them to make the Imperial Crown of India. It contains almost 6,000 precious stones and is, intrinsically, probably the most valuable crown. It was worn by King George V only for the Delhi Durbar and has not been used since.

THE CROWN OF QUEEN ELIZABETH THE QUEEN MOTHER

This Crown is unusual, being the only one made of platinum. It was created for Queen Elizabeth the Queen Mother in 1937. The arches can be removed and the circlet worn alone. The principal diamond, set in the Maltese Cross at the front of the Crown, is the Koh-i-noor (Mountain of Light).

The legend of the Koh-i-noor goes back some 3,000 years but, although this diamond is the oldest of the major diamonds, it is unlikely to be older than the seventeenth century. It was almost

A detail from G.P. Jacomb-Hood's watercolour (1912) of George V wearing the Imperial Crown of India at the Delhi Durbar in 1911

Imperial Crown of India, 1911

certainly found in 1655 at the Kollur Mine in the Golconda region of India. The diamond was presented to Shah Jahan in Shahjahanabad and remained there until 1739 when it went to Isfahan in Persia after the sack of Delhi by Nadir Shah. After a long, chequered history it went via Northern Persia to Afghanistan and thence back to India. After Britain annexed the Punjab in 1849, the diamond was presented to Queen Victoria in 1850 by the East India Company.

When originally found, the diamond weighed some 787 carats but was ground down disgracefully by a Venetian cutter, Hortensio Borgio, and was only 280 carats when weighed by Jean-Baptiste Tavernier in 1665. Some time later, it must have been cut again as it weighed 186 carats on arrival in England. At that time it was mounted with two other diamonds in the form of an upper arm bracelet and there are pictures of Ranjit Singh, the Lion of the Punjab, wearing it in that manner. Prince Albert, Queen Victoria's consort, disliked the Indian cut and, after careful consideration, it was decided to re-cut to a brilliant, bringing it down to its present weight of 106 carats.

As the murky history of the diamond involves brothers blinding brothers it is thought to be unlucky for a man to wear it. Consequently, it is placed in the Queen Consort's Crown.

Sir Gerald Kelly's portrait (c1938) of Queen Elizabeth the Queen Mother. The Koh-i-noor Diamond is set in the Maltese Cross at the front of her Crown

Royal Collection

QUEEN MARY'S CROWN

This Crown was designed for Queen Mary to wear at the Coronation in 1911. In the centre of the Maltese Cross at the front is a large, oval crystal interchangeable with the Koh-i-noor Diamond now set in Queen Elizabeth the Queen Mother's Crown. The third and fourth largest stones of the Cullinan Diamond were also set in this Crown but they have now been replaced by crystals, and the diamonds have reverted to the personal possession of the Queen. It is in the traditional style, set in silver with a gold back.

THE SMALL CROWN OF QUEEN VICTORIA

Made in 1870 from diamonds taken from a fringe necklace, this Crown is in the traditional style and mounted in silver and gold. It weighs approximately 4 oz (113 gr) and a bun hair style was required to wear it. Queen Victoria was very fond of it and is seen wearing it in most of the representations of her after the age of fifty-one. It is said that she disliked the Imperial State Crown because, being a small woman, she

Coloured engraving (1900) after Benjamin Constant of Queen Victoria wearing her Small Crown at the Palace of Westminster

Royal Library

The Crown of Queen Elizabeth the
Queen Mother, 1937

Queen Mary's Crown, 1911

The Small Crown of Queen
Victoria, 1870

The Crown of Mary of Modena, 1685

The Diadem of Mary of Modena, 1685

William Wissing's portrait (c1685) of Mary of Modena

National Portrait Gallery

found it clumsy and the procedures of getting it out of the Jewel House too cumbersome for her liking.

——: THE CROWN OF MARY OF MODENA :——

Again, it is interesting to imagine the hair style required to wear this Crown as it is only 5 in (127 mm) across. Mounted in silver and gold and set with crystals and cultured pearls, it is one of the crowns often set with precious stones which were removed after a Coronation and replaced by crystals. The Crown was last worn by Queen Charlotte, wife of King George III. Associated with it is the Diadem of Mary of Modena, also set with crystals and cultured pearls. In the same fashion as the Crown, these were replaced by precious stones at the time of a Coronation, the Diadem being last worn by Queen Adelaide. The purpose of this Crown and Diadem can be confusing because the Coronation Crown of Mary of Modena is not held in the Tower, although the frame is on display at the Museum of London. Mary of Modena went to Westminster Abbey wearing the Diadem, was then crowned with the Coronation Crown, and left wearing the Crown described above, which is on display with the other

The Prince of Wales Crown, 1728

The Prince of Wales Crown, 1901

Crown Jewels at the Tower of London. It was the Consort's equivalent to the Imperial State Crown.

——•: THE PRINCE OF WALES CROWN 1728 :•——

Made for Prince Frederick Louis, the son of King George II, this Crown was used when he took his seat in the House of Lords where it was placed on a cushion in front of him. It was used subsequently in the same fashion, lastly by King Edward VII when Prince of Wales. It has never been used since.

——•: THE PRINCE OF WALES CROWN 1901 :•——

This Crown was made for Prince George, later King George V, for the Coronation of King Edward VII in 1902. It was also worn by Edward Prince of Wales (later King Edward VIII and subsequently Duke of Windsor) at the Coronation of King George V in 1911.

THE BANQUETING PLATE

After a Coronation, it was customary to hold a Coronation Banquet. King George IV was determined that his banquet should excel all others. Typical of some of the Banqueting Plate are the two ornate dish warmers, each with two spirit lamps underneath to keep the food warm. Coronation Banquets were discontinued after the 1821 feast and the Banqueting Plate in the Jewel House is therefore no longer used. There are several major items and the importance of salt in olden days is highlighted by the number of Salts (salt cellars) on display.

THE EXETER SALT c1630

The City of Exeter had supported Parliament against King Charles I. On the Restoration of King Charles II the City Fathers wanted to present the King with a gift to help restore them to his favour. They purchased this very complicated Salt, generally attributed to Johann Hass of Hamburg. Many theories have been expounded about the design but it is doubtful whether any have great significance.

The Salt consists of a castle which forms the lower half, the upper half being remarkably like the old Pharos (lighthouse) of Alexandria, the seventh wonder of the world. Engravings of the Pharos of Alexandria circulated in Germany at the time that the Exeter Salt was made and one may have been used as a basis for this unusual design. All the turrets can be removed and underneath each is a small receptacle which holds about an ounce of salt.

Dish Warmer and Cover

The Exeter Salt, c1630

There are also a drawbridge and drawers used for pepper, English saffron, cloves, cinnamon and so on. The Salt would have been placed in front of the Sovereign and the rank of a guest would decide where he sat in relation to it.

FOUNTAIN AND PERFUME BURNER c 1650

The City Fathers of Plymouth, like those of Exeter, had supported Cromwell. Also wishing to gain favour with

Fountain and Perfume Burner, c1650

Charles II they presented him with this Fountain on his Restoration. Generally attributed to Peter Oehr I of Hamburg it was originally silver, was first gilded in 1727 and re-gilded in 1821 for the Coronation of King George IV. It is a Fountain with liquid coming out of the top figure and the four figures around the stem, the liquid being fed by gravity from a tank or barrel. The liquid was probably perfumed water. The top figure used to be that of Hercules but, after the Coronation of King George III, Prince Frederick Ernst, a Page of the Back Stairs at Buckingham Palace, did not return it to the Jewel House. A new figure representing Cleopatra and the Asp had to be made for the Coronation of King George IV.

ST GEORGE'S SALTS 1661

The probable origin of these Salts was a banquet organised by the Knights of the Garter on 15 April 1661, in honour of St George's Day, at which King Charles II was present. Four

Sir Thomas Lawrence's portrait (1821) of George IV. The Fountain and Perfume Burner were re-gilded for his Coronation in 1821

Queen Elizabeth I Salt Cellar, 1572

King Charles II Salt Cellar, 1661

Salts of hourglass shape were made for the King's Table and four separate sets of four, of cylinder type, for the Knights' Tables or Messes. All these Salts had canopies with a horse and rider on top.

A set of four more was made for Officers of the Order who were not Knights of the Garter. These Salts had napkin brackets round the salt well instead of canopies. It is probable that twelve Salts of cylinder type were melted down by Sir Gilbert Talbot in 1680 when King Charles II was running short of money. Another of cylinder type disappeared at the time of the Coronation of King William and Queen Mary in 1689. It may be at this time that the Queen Elizabeth Salt (1572) was added to make up numbers. Although so called it is by no means certain that it belonged to Queen Elizabeth I but it is a beautiful piece of silver-gilt of that period.

At the Coronation of King George IV, the Crown Jewellers of the day mistook the brackets for legs on the four Salts of the Officers of the Order. They turned the Salts upside down and made new salt containers. These Salts were therefore displayed upside down for nearly a hundred years

Portrait (c1690) by an unknown artist of William III

until, in 1906, William Watts of the Victoria & Albert Museum pointed out the error.

It is possible that the name St George's Salts originated from Sir Henry St George, the Garter King of Arms, who organised the St George's Day feast in 1696, rather than from the more obvious connection with St George's Day. Before 1696, they bore no special name.

❧ THE CADDINETS ❧

The origin of the word is probably the old French "Cadenas" which was a place setting containing the table utensils of royalty or very high nobility. The earliest reference to them is in 1549. Because of their restricted use by persons of rank, they could and did cause awkward problems of etiquette.

The first Caddinet was made in 1683 and its William and Mary Coat of Arms must have been added at a later date. The second, made in 1689, was one of two made partly from old plate and partly from an old Caddinet. The Coat of Arms is of particular interest as the second and third quarters are both occupied by the Irish Harp while the second supporter is not the Scottish Unicorn but the Tudor Dragon. The explanation is that the English Parliament offered the Crown to King William and Queen Mary on 13 February

Portrait, unknown date, after William Wissing of Mary II

Caddinet, 1683

1689 whereas the Scottish Parliament did not meet until 4 March, the Coronation being on 11 April. There was no certainty that the Scots would follow the English and it was, therefore, proper, or tactful, to have no allusion to Scotland during this, the "no Scottish" period.

The two Caddinets on display were probably sold with other old plate in 1808 to defray the expenses of the Princess of Wales, Caroline of Brunswick. Some plate went to Lowther Castle and came into the possession of the Earl of Lonsdale. The Caddinets were acquired jointly by Queen Elizabeth II and the Government from Lord Lonsdale's estate and went on display in the Jewel House in 1975.

THE WINE COOLER 1829

This was made in the last year of King George IV's reign, to the design of John Bridge. It has a Greek theme with the ocean in the form of a sea cave encrusted with shells, lobsters and seaweed supporting rocks and earth on which grows a rich vineyard with children playing. It is said to hold 144 bottles of claret. The wine was cooled by ice and damp cloths, claret being not necessarily served at room temperature in those days. It is extremely heavy, weighing 8,000 ounces, or nearly a quarter of a ton (255 kg). Queen Victoria decided to use it as a Punch Bowl for the christening of her eldest son, later to become King Edward VII, and for this purpose a ladle, the bowl of which represents a large conch shell, was made in 1841.

The Wine Cooler or Grand Punch Bowl, 1829

OTHER CHURCH PLATE

A variety of Church Plate is on display, some more important than others. Typical of the time of the Restoration are the three pairs of feathered flagons dated 1660 or 1664.

The pair of large silver-gilt candlesticks, circa 1662, can be associated with the interesting history of Fortnum & Mason of Piccadilly. William Fortnum was a footman to

Candlesticks, c1662

Queen Anne and one of his "fringe benefits" was the disposal of used candle ends from all the royal candlesticks. He sold them to Hugh Mason, a grocer in Piccadilly. Later, his grandson, Charles Fortnum, who was a footman to Queen Charlotte, the wife of King George III, cemented this relationship on his retirement from Royal service by joining the Mason family to form Fortnum & Mason. To this day, if you watch the clock strike the hour outside Fortnum & Mason, you will see two figures of men emerge from it, one bearing a salver and the other bearing a candelabra.

➤ ALTAR DISH 1691 ➤

Perhaps the finest silver-gilt Dish on display is that made by Francis Garthorne. With the accompanying Flagon, it was given in 1691 to Lord Lucas, then Constable of the Tower. The Flagon was made by either Samuel Hood or Samuel Hawkes, their mark being the same. These pieces belong to

Feathered Flagons, 1664

The Maundy Dish, 1660

the Chapel of St Peter ad Vincula, the Royal Chapel within the Tower, and are placed on its altar every Christmas, Easter and Whitsun. The motif on the Dish is thought to be the Feast of Emmaus. Also displayed is another Altar Dish of similar size, dated 1660, although the cypher on it is clearly that of Queen Anne. This apparent inconsistency can be confusing but often the cypher was either changed or put on at a later date.

❧ THE MAUNDY DISH 1660 ❧

On Maundy Thursday (the Thursday before Easter), the Sovereign presents the Maundy Money, which is specially minted, to old age pensioners selected by the Bishop, at a different cathedral every year. The money is of one, two, three and four pence in silver, although the Sovereign also gives some modern money as well. The number of pensioners equates to the Sovereign's age at the time.

The present ceremony dates from the time of King Charles II but a form of it has taken place as far back as we

Her Majesty the Queen distributing the Maundy Money

Altar Dish, 1691

have records. It follows the Biblical theme of humility and washing the feet of the poor.

The Maundy Dish has the cypher of King William and Queen Mary and, like the Caddinets, is of the "no Scottish" period as it is clear that there are two Irish Harps and no Scottish Lion. As the age of the present Queen does not allow room for all the packages to be placed on the Maundy Dish it is augmented by the "Fish Dishes", two altar dishes, circa 1661, which have a fish motif in the centre. They are of continental origin. Nowadays when the Queen presents the Maundy Money at an inland cathedral the dish with fresh-water fish displayed is sent out; when the cathedral is on or close to the coast the dish with sea-water fish is selected.

Altar Dish, c1685

THE CHRISTENING FONTS

King Charles II came to the throne unmarried. He persuaded the Treasury to pay for a Christening Font, now known as the King Charles II Font, as he said he was going to marry a Spanish princess. If necessary, it could be held by the Spanish Ambassador. In the event, he married a Portuguese princess, Catherine of Braganza by whom he had no children. He retained the Font and it is said that it was used to christen some of his illegitimate children, of which he had at least thirteen. The first Sovereign to be christened in the Font was King George IV, but it was used by members of the Royal Family up to the time of the christening of Queen Victoria herself. The two

King Charles II Christening Font and Altar Dish, 1660

One of the Tankards attributed to Hieronymus Hass, c1650

Tankards circa 1650 associated with it and generally attributed to Habs Lambrecht III of Hamburg are embossed with Bacchanalian scenes of high relief figures.

There is a Ewer and Basin circa 1735 which was used for the christening of King George III at Norfolk House. His father, Prince Frederick Louis, was in disgrace at the time and banished from the Court of King George II, so being denied the use of the King Charles II Font.

Ewer and Basin, c1735

➤ THE LILY CHRISTENING FONT 1840 ➤

This was made by E J & W Barnard on the orders of Queen Victoria and there is a possibility that Prince Albert was closely concerned with the design. The Coats of Arms of Queen Victoria, and the joint Arms of Queen Victoria and Prince Albert and the Princess Royal are on it. It was said that Queen Victoria did not care for the King Charles II Christening Font because of the links with King Charles II's illegitimate children or its flagons because of their pagan subjects.

The Lily Font is a delightful piece of silver-gilt and is the one used by the Royal Family today. Whenever it is used, the 1735 Ewer goes with it.

The Lily Christening Font, 1840

·MEDALS· AND ORDERS OF CHIVALRY

A complete collection of decorations and medals awarded from 1900 to 1982 is also on display. In addition, there is a selection of Coronation, Jubilee, Efficiency and Long Service medals. The orders of chivalry and the robes associated with them are also shown. The senior of them, the Most Noble Order of the Garter, was founded by King Edward III in 1348. It consists of twenty-six members including the Sovereign and Consort. The robes of this Order are particularly well known from the portrait of Queen Elizabeth II by Annigoni.

Edward III was noted for his chivalry and it is said that the Order originated in an incident at a ball in Calais where he was dancing with his cousin, Joan, Countess of Salisbury, also known as the Fair Maid of Kent. Unfortunately, she dropped her garter and as she was embarrassed the King picked it up, pinned it to his left knee and uttered the famous phrase "Honi soit qui mal y pense" which can be roughly translated as "Evil be to him who evil thinks". He then decided to institute the Order.

Other orders displayed are the Order of the Thistle, the Order of the Bath, the Order of St Michael and St George, the Royal Victorian Order and the Order of the

The tomb effigy in Westminster Abbey of Edward III, who founded the Most Noble Order of the Garter in 1348

Dean and Chapter, Westminster Abbey

Victoria Cross

Pietro Annigoni's portrait (1954-55) of Her Majesty the Queen wearing the Garter Robes

The Robes of the Royal Victorian Order

British Empire. The Order of the Bath, founded in 1399 by King Henry IV on his accession, also has an interesting history. King Henry's friends, who were to escort him to his Coronation, took a bath in the Chapel of St John in the White Tower at the Tower of London the night before the Coronation. The King marked a cross in water on their backs and after this formed the Order of the Bath.

Also displayed, but no longer in use, are the Order of St Patrick, the Order of the Star of India and the Order of the Indian Empire.

⤙ POSTSCRIPT ⤙

Are they real and what are they worth? One man who was quite certain that they were real and that they were worth stealing was Colonel Blood, an Irish renegade, who in 1671 made the only attempt to steal the Crown Jewels. Posing as a clergyman he got to know Talbot Edwards, the Keeper of the Crown Jewels. Blood persuaded Edwards that his nephew might make a good match for Edwards' daughter and they arranged an appointment early one morning to discuss the matter. Blood arrived with two accomplices and, whilst they were waiting for Mrs Edwards to appear, he suggested that they went to look at the Crown Jewels. Edwards lived in the Martin Tower and the Crown Jewels were kept on the ground floor. He was not paid a salary but was entitled to show people the Crown Jewels on payment.

Edwards took Blood and his accomplices into the room where the Crown Jewels were held. He was struck on the head and, because he made so much noise, was also stabbed. The thieves rushed off with the Crown, the Sceptre and the Orb but were unfortunate in that Edwards' son, an Army officer, arrived home unexpectedly on leave and raised the alarm. Blood and his accomplices were caught at the East Gate of the Tower and in the confusion the Orb rolled into the gutter. Later, Blood was pardoned and pensioned by King Charles II for reasons which remain obscure. Nobody will ever know why King Charles II followed the legend of the Curtana Sword and chose "mercy rather than revenge".

Etching, artist and date unknown, of Colonel Blood